Shedding Childhood

Katie Hemel

BookLeaf
Publishing

India | USA | UK

Presentation by *BookLeaf Publishing*

Web: www.bookleafpub.com

E-mail: info@bookleafpub.com

ISBN: 9789358314328

First edition 2023

DEDICATION

For any survivor, may you find your voice and
speak your truth.

ACKNOWLEDGEMENT

To Brian, Thank you for always giving me the creative space to be myself in my forever journey of self-expression, healing, and knowing myself. I love you and our family more than words.

To my children, It is my greatest honor to be your mother. My forever wish is to meet you with the best version of myself and to always protect you from any sort of harm.

To my parents and sisters, I am forever grateful I was blessed with you. I would not trade a second of my past if it also meant losing you.

To my grandmother, In life and after death, I have always felt your support and love. Thank you for never backing down on your encouragement to write.

To Ashleigh, Thank you for reading thousands of my words. I could not ask for a better writing partner, nor a better friend. I cannot wait until roles are reversed, and I am reading your novel.

Kelly and Jennifer, I live for our girls' dinners. Your support during my life, but especially during this time of midlife, means the world to me.

To all my other dear friends, Thank you for letting me share my story and listening without judgment. You have given me the courage to take back my power.

PREFACE

On Tuesdays in second grade, I walked to my grandparents' home after school. It was a perk of being the oldest– for one day a week, I got to skip my after school childcare and spend the afternoon with my grandmother reading books, forever drawing, and eating ice cream sandwiches. On one particular walk home, I met a girl who lived across the street from my grandmother. We began playing regularly on Tuesdays, either at my grandmother's or at the neighborhood park. As our young friendship deepened, she began to create new games for us to play. Sometimes we wove together friendship bracelets or chased each other with endless child energy, and sometimes she convinced me to pretend to be her wife fast asleep in bed, so she could kiss my neck to wake me up. Sometimes she convinced me to take my clothes off, and when I resisted, she assured me everyone did it. Although intermittent, this type of "play" continued for the next four years. But it wasn't solely the ongoing reactivity that hurt, but also the tighter manipulation and control she gained over me, which continued into young adulthood. One of the most pivotal moments occurred at a mutual friend's wedding when she slapped my

ass and said, "Just like when we were little."
However, there were also plenty of fun times
intermingled throughout. She was the first to
brag that I could flip the entirety of the park.
There were trips to the local fair, all the drives to
school and home as we got older, and the times
when I did feel I could trust her. It was very
confusing for me as a child, adolescent, and
young adult. While I harbored anger long into
adulthood, I still maintained a relationship with
her into our forties.

In reflection, it is almost unbelievable how the
cycle of power and control creeps in, and how
the fear of repercussions of cutting ties can still
hold a tight rein long after the childhood years
have passed. In addition, the two times I had the
courage to share a small detail of my story, it
had been repeatedly minimized to "a simple
game of doctor." At age forty-one, by divine
intervention, I read the book, *Daring Greatly*, by
Brene Brown with the line, "When you own
your story, you get to write the ending." That
single line changed the trajectory of my entire
life up until that point. Within a couple short
weeks of reading this line, I found a wonderful
therapist that helped me begin my journey of
healing.

The Shame We Carry

To the girl that reacted her own sexual abuse on to me,

Remember how in high school, sentimental gifts were
a requirement of my friendship to you? How I had to
wander the aisles of Carlton Cards searching for the perfect
quote on cheap cardstock with a picture of a nature scene?
I could not even tell my parents I loved them, and yet,
I was supposed to tell you. The shame that came with
telling you, my violator, this, when all I really desired was
the strength to dissolve our relationship,
buried itself deeply and found a home within my soul for
far too long, but it is no longer welcome here.
So, let this letter serve as my last, most sincere gift of all.

Remember when we were seven and you coaxed me
to lie on the ground at my grandmother's house?
You asked me to pretend to sleep, so you could wake me by
kissing my neck. You said we were having sex.
I protested, but you told me all the kids in school did it.
I didn't know the difference, so I just laid there,
wondering if other kids felt the same discomfort.
This first occasion started 34 years of self-disgust, and
I'm gifting it back to you.

Remember when you made me lie naked in the bathtub
and you climbed on top? The feel of the cool porcelain
against my back as you stuck your tongue in my mouth,
is a memory I've desperately tried to erase.
The weakness and filth that washed over me that day,
coated my skin for all the years that followed.
My repulsion of your smell…your touch…your taste…
I'm gifting them back to you.

Remember around eleven when you made me reenact
the Love is Strange scene from Dirty Dancing?
I knew we were too old to still be doing this.
By that time, I no longer verbally protested,
but I assure you every fiber of my being did.
The yearning to wipe away your unsolicited touches,
the need to reconcile why this continued to happen,
which has haunted me ever since,
I'm gifting them back to you.

Do you remember when, on my behalf—but
without my consent—you asked the boys to the eighth
grade dance and they all said "no"? I remember well
the next day at school, as they glanced in my direction
and began to whisper. I sank low into my desk,
cheeks burning red, and began my life-long habit of
counting the ways their "nos" were justified. The years
that followed of never feeling smart enough, pretty enough,
or desirable enough to be liked,
I'm gifting them back to you.

Do you remember at your middle school slumber party
when you dared me to tell my Major secret to all
the girls? When I refused, you took them outside
and told them anyway. The humiliation I felt as
they all came back in, staring in disgust at
the-girl-who-had-once-touched-herself-over-her-clothes,
likely a direct result of what you had done, never went
away. The years of mortification of walking through a
hallway where everyone knows your darkest secret, and the
subsequent confusion of learning my own body,
I'm gifting them back to you.

Do you remember in high school making fun of the hairs
on my lip, or how pale my skin is?
Do you remember calling my nose wide and my feet big?

The years of not looking someone in the face while
speaking, for fear they notice my flawed face; or
refusing to wear shorts, though it was far too hot for pants;
or spending an ungodly amount of time staring at my
disproportionate feet;
I'm gifting them back to you.

I know at seven it was not your fault,
and there is a part of me that aches for you as a
three-year-old, a victim yourself. But, at what age were
you accountable?
Was it 11?...14?...17?
I do not have an answer,
but I know damn well there was no innocence behind your
26-year-old self that slapped my ass at a
mutual friend's wedding and declared,
"Just like when we were little."
This moment confirmed everything I had ever questioned.
In this second, I realized the breadth of your manipulation
and depth of intentionality, and
I'm gifting them all back to you.

I've taken each of these gifts
and every countless one in between;
I've delicately unwrapped them one by one,
analyzed them from every angle and held them in the light.
Their chains within me are slowly corroding—loosening—
and it is time now for you to take them.
So, please, accept each toxic, sordid one.

They were never mine to begin with.

Thief

As a latchkey kid of the 80's and the oldest of three,
I became the mother for two hours each afternoon at
the age of nine, Mondays-Fridays,
while Mom and Dad worked.
I never claim to have been a good mother—
More of an annoyed, hateful mother toward my two
sisters, but in charge of snacks and safety,
nonetheless. A badge of pride I wear to this day;
validation of my gen-x-fuck-you attitude.

Many kids carried their house keys in their backpacks
then. It was as common as Guess and Benetton.
One day my abuser, a childhood peer I considered a
friend at the time, asked where I kept my key.
A trusting eleven-year-old, I unzipped the front
pouch of my bag to show her.
How was I to know she would slip it
into her pocket 10 minutes later?
That she would sneak into our home in a few days
to steal my life savings stashed under my bed,
while our family visited North Carolina?

A message blinking red on the answering machine
from the mother of a friend, whom she had confided
in, waited for us when we arrived home.
Mom immediately directed me to check my cash box.
Confirmed empty, she called my abuser's Dad. They
walked over to deliver the money

and an apology to my parents.
I crept down the stairs and listened through the wall.
Mom demanded "why";
my abuser muttered "sorry".
Mom was angry—protective of me—
it was palpable and fleeting.
A feeling of safety I yearned for in the years to come.

How was Mom to know this wasn't the first time my
abuser stole from me?
That she ripped away my innocence at
seven-years-old, when she kissed my neck
for the first of many times?
Where was my protector then?
My proverbial older sister?
My Mother?
Mom never knew until 34 years later,
when I finally summoned the courage to tell her.

For years, I pondered how the anger and refuge were
lost on this. Had it merely slipped through the hands
of hardworking parents doing their best to rear their
children in the best neighborhood, with the best
schools?
What does privilege matter, when it's steeped in
trauma?
When your neighbor across the street comes to play
daily and sometimes the play is naked and invasive?

It took three decades to understand that of all the
possessions my abuser stole, my forgiveness and
capacity to love my Mother wholeheartedly, were

among the most precious of all. My abuser robbed
these from deep inside my soul without my knowing.
She reached in—like the cunning,
deviant eleven-year-old version of herself
taking the key to my home—
and left only bitterness and anger to fester.

I am my own protector now, replenished of love and
forgiveness. I collected every ounce of the displaced
anger and cultivated it into a poem detailing my
trauma. Once ready, I sealed it in an envelope
addressed to my abuser's home
and drove to the post office—a sense of liberation
coursing through my veins.
As the letter fell deep into the blue box, it echoed….

It was not Mom's fault.
It was never Mom's fault.

She was just easy to blame.

My Mother's Love

Dear Mom,

One night, around age sixteen,
you crawled into my bed and leaned in,
holding a thick white card embossed with teal
foil writing. You asked me to listen as you read
a poem about a free-spirited daughter with blond
curls and a mother who fiercely loved the tiny
child her daughter once was— and the woman
she was becoming.
I'm sure you sat in the silence afterward waiting
for me to speak, and when I didn't,
you left.

What you don't know is I remember that
moment like it was yesterday. I knew it
was a lifeline to pull me back into our
family, and I've held close to that
moment to help light the consuming
darkness I've felt throughout the years.

What you don't know is when I turned seven,
my abuser reacted her own molestation
on me, and, as we got older, it continued
but with threats of retaliation

in the worst of childhood ways.
She held my head under in that
whirlpool of trauma, and I was
too ashamed to thrash around.

What you don't know is
it was all I could do to gasp for air—
to grasp for control—
through food, obsessive thoughts, and deep cuts.
The anger makes so much sense now.

But what you need to know—
what you must know—
is the card you gave me in that moment of pure
love, has been far more reaching and
far more powerful than any
whirlpool could have ever been.

Borrowed Love

Before I learned to stand on my own,
to love myself first, which to me, means
choosing short term hurt instead of
prolonged pain trying to prove my love
to someone who never wanted it to begin with,
I stood for years on the borrowed strength of
three other women--
On their borrowed legs and borrowed love.

The home of my childhood babysitter, Lindy,
always felt the safest to me, despite the
second-hand smoke, bottomless sweet tea
quenching my thirst, and pet turtle carrying
God-knows-what-bacteria walking around.
Here I could be myself, as
Lindy would remind me,
"We all put our pants on one leg at a time."
She knew and loved all my quirks, and though
I've never known exactly where I fit,
I always fit perfectly there.

Aunt Susan reminded me you're funny, wild,
and free already, you just have to tap into it.

"Who cares if you have imperfections on your
face. So does your sister and she's beautiful.
Same thing for your mom. Here, take a
drink…listen to this joke….and let's laugh...
See, it's fun to escape this way….
Nothing's ever serious, and you can find this fun
in these vices whenever
you don't feel it on your own."

Grandmother Margaret says creativity and
self-expression are important, and she modeled
that with her watercolor paintings and
hand-crafted nativity scenes made from shells
found along the beaches of Florida.
"You don't have to be perfect, but you sure
have a gift and stories to tell, so promise me,
you'll take some classes and
keep on writing."

I've carried these women with me all my life.
I've borrowed their secret ingredients
over and over, on borrowed time.
I'm learning these gifts were always within me
to begin with.

And, on the days, when memories of trauma
surface and whisper in my ear, like a demon on
my shoulder,
"You are not enough. You are not worthy",

I know I can turn to the heavens and beg for
these women's blessings again, and the
heavens will respond just as freely as they
always have...
"Child, here is your refuge, here is your escape,
and here is your expression.
These are the gifts of your ancestors.
These are your gifts of love.
And this love is constant
even when you cannot feel it."

Thin

Before it was trendy, I studied applied
behavior analysis. I learned intermittent
reinforcement is the strongest of all–it's
the reason we play the lottery, after all. When
we get a positive response on occasion, we keep
coming back for the good stuff, time and time
again, knowing sometimes a reward will be
waiting. It's also the reason, I learned, years later
in therapy that my tendency toward
obsessive-compulsive disorder morphed
into an eating disorder. When you have
little control over the rumors that are spread
and can never seem to sever the friendship
with the person that touched you over and
over again without your consent, you begin
to tune out the real world and make
up your own head games to control.

The rules are simple and blurry, written with
desperation and kept safely deep within the
lines of teenage journals. Only a bowl of
cereal for breakfast, lunch, and dinner,
and you'll get that A. Only five pounds
to lose, and he will certainly say
"hi" in the hallway today. Two

diet cokes and a piece of
wheat bread, and he will
like you back. But as
the game continues
the rules get stricter-
the meals smaller-
you thinner.
And you realize
You're playing
This game
All
Alone

Poker

The first time I ever spoke of my abuse,
I was 17 and shared just a little with my friend.
A single card of my royal flush in a poker
match, with ten years' worth of chips on the
table. She told me it was normal and
all kids play this game of doctor.

I picked up my cards, placed them back in the
deck, and swept the chips right into my
backpack. This game had to end early. Neither of
us really knew the rules, and I was certain there
would be no winners this round.

I carried the deck and chips around for 20 more
years searching for someone who might know
the rules, someone patient enough to teach me. I
sometimes wondered if poker games were worth
the trouble to learn anyway, but

I mostly wondered what was wrong with me
for making such a big deal out of
such a common game to begin with.

Birthday Party

For Alex,

I knew God and the angels watched over me when it
did not rain during my outdoor wedding,
despite a thunderstorm risk of 75-percent.
Five years later when my eldest was born,
they were there again.

He was due the 29th, and aside from the usual
prayers of health, the daily prayer became, please let
him come any day but the 27th, my abuser's birthday.
Between every doctor's appointment
and baby shower was a
prayer for him to have a birthday devoid of the evil
the 27th represented to me. How could my
perfect baby boy share it with her?

When labor started at 4 a.m. on the 26th,
I felt relief, but labor was slow,
and true to character, he took his sweet time.
With each passing hour,
the prayers became more urgent:
Dear God, please don't make me reconcile this day—
please don't make me have to tell myself he
represents the yang to this ying—
that beauty and innocence can still be found
within evil.
Please God, don't juxtaposition my precious boy
against her manipulation and disgust.

I don't want to spend a lifetime
in this mental hell.

As three hours of pushing started to close in on the
midnight deadline, my prayers became pleads:
Please God, keep her out of this room.
Please God, no, why is she always here?
How does she creep in, even during one of the
happiest moments of my life?
Please God, extract her from this birth
and my memory all together.

And God and the angels listened.
At 11:04 p.m., with 56 minutes to spare,
My sweet son was here.
And every birthday celebration thereafter—
every party, every candle,
every bite of cake, and
every year of pride,
she is
not.

Never has there been,
nor will there ever be,
an invitation for her.

Pendulum

For Anna,

Don't we all want to give our children the
things we did not have in our own childhood?
For my daughter, it's ongoing permission to cut
and style her Barbies' hair. It's the pack of
gum in the checkout line at Target and the
occasional ice cream for dinner. It's the "good"
clothes for back to school. It's summer
excursions across the country and
late winter road trips to Mardi Gras.

It's a hope she knows she can choose sports and
arts, but they will never solely define her.
That she can love boys, girls, both, or none,
and it is all up to her.
That she can love God, yet
still question anything she wants.
That she can wear striped shorts and polka-dot
shirts together any day of the week.

It's a hope that when she thinks of her
childhood, it's as warm and comforting as a quilt
woven together with the thousands of beautifully
colored affirmations she's been
whispered since birth:

smart, funny, resilient, authentic, creative,
kind, athletic, innocent, brave, and
so very, very loved.

It's a prayer for a childhood unlike mine.
A prayer for a childhood not stained with abuse.
A prayer for the childhood I deserved.

Two Pillowcases

My abuser gave me two pillowcases
as a wedding gift.
The thread count so high, they
felt like satin against my cheeks. For 15 years,
every time I laid to sleep, I thought of her.
I thought of the sexual reactivity—
the bullying—
the name calling—
the rumor spreading—
the stealing.
I thought of the control she had over me,
and wondered exactly where on the spectrum
of shame and fear laid her wedding invitation
to begin with.
The memory of her tainted
every fiber of those thousands of threads.

And then, one day, after years
of therapy to reconcile my history,
I threw them out.
It was a simple walk to the trash can.
Short and without ritual.
An action so much bigger than the moment.

I could sleep on sandpaper or silk

now and it would not matter.
My tired is good and welcome,
and when my cheek hits the pillow
there is no thought—
just eyes
closing.

Wandering

"Let go or be dragged"
   --Zen Proverb

I let her drag me for 30 years
by the hair, face down in the dirt.
She pulled and pulled me.
Sometimes over rocks and roots that cut so
deeply into my skin it made me
fearful to face the world.
Sometimes, when she felt nice,
she would let me rest and tell
me how good I was for letting her
drag me down. "Oh, Katie,
you're the only one who understands
me. Thank you for your loyalty.
You're my best friend."
And, when I got too comfortable, she would
pull me over rocks and roots again, so I
could not remember how to protest.

Then one day I mustered the courage to try to
stand. And, when I realized I could,
I squinted against the brilliant light of
the sun and pushed her away.

She ran and never looked back, and I, with
barely the strength of only a toddler, started to
step. I have no idea if my steps were forward,
sideways, or backward, and I know for certain
there were trips and falls,
but at least, despite
wherever I was heading,
even if only circles in the same spot,
it was the journey
of my choosing now.

Goldfish

Before Brian, I likened
myself to a goldfish circling
round and round in a glass bowl.
My life no bigger than
a 10-mile radius.
I often listened to
Wish You Were Here by Pink Floyd on repeat,
belting out the line
"We're just two lost souls
swimming in a fish bowl
year after year…",
with an all-too-familiar-understanding.
Except in my version,
I was the only fish,
with only a plastic plant
keeping me company.

A week after meeting Brian,
He said, "Hey baby, let's go to Mardi Gras"
And we did.

Then he said, "Let's move to FL….
to NOLA…
to NC…
to Nashville…"
And we did.

He said, "Let's travel to Costa Rica…
to Norway…
to Mexico…
to Puerto Rico…
and let's keep going and going and
going to new places."
And we did.

He said, "Let's make the most of this life,
because the same thing on repeat is boring
and this life is too short to be bored."

He said, "Hey baby, take my hand
and my heart and let's make a life together.
Let's dance and have fun and
laugh and laugh and laugh."
And we did.

We did all of those and more.
For years, he helped me escape
until I realized it was time to circle back
to home.
To my therapist.
To my fish bowl.
To learn to be happy
swimming alone,
keeping my own company.

Shedding Childhood

Peaches, our Gecko, came to us
as a gift for my son almost five years ago.
Until recently we never saw her shedding skin,
something that occurs every month or so.
Geckos prefer to shed in the dead of night and
eat the dead skin all before the next sunrise.
So, last week, when my daughter yelled
for me to look at Peaches,
with such an urgency, I could only assume
she had quietly passed in her aquarium home, I
came rushing. When I entered the room,
Peaches was alive and well, but still
undressing her dried skin.
She had started from the top and pushed
the dead layer halfway down her scaly back,
revealing vivid spots on her upper half
where the dulled skin had been just hours before,
preparing to release. She noticed us watching
and immediately hid under her rock, as if
embarrassed, and I couldn't help but empathize.

After years of wearing dulled skin and hiding
my abuse, once I began to peel away the layers,
I emerged with a new light.
But newborn skin is thin and fragile, and

sometimes you feel naked with your new colors
shining brightly for everyone to see.

Antidote

Healing myself is
as simple as learning
value lies somewhere on the
spectrum of
authenticity and vulnerability,
in my actions and words.

Healing myself is
as simple as unlearning
that worth isn't found within
beauty and achievements,
athleticism and grades,
careers and money,
using a measuring stick
of others' accomplishments.

Healing myself is
creativity and writing,
therapy and health,
instead of dreaming a fantasy world
full of accolades
and wishing them true.

Ankylosaurus

It's a fact, psychologists say,
the body holds the trauma,
even if the mind does not remember. Even
when the mind tries to forget.

While I could never forget my
sexual abuse, I tried to bury it deep within,
too scared and ashamed
to disclose it.

That must be what abuse does,
when it's pushed deep into the body.
It must climb into the weakest crevices and
most tired parts and claim it as home
until we evict it.

For me, this was the spine.
Thirty years it held my head high,
even when I wanted to bow in shame.
It held my shoulders back,
and helped me walk,
despite my personal preference for the fetal
position. One foot in front of the other,
step after step after step.
And, I suppose, after years of working hard

to stay upright and
fighting a constant war against
the body's desire to crumble,
eventually it gets tired.
Eventually it saves itself by
simplyfusing.

I'm an Ankylosaurus now,
the fun name given to those of us with
Ankylosing Spondylitis. The name
of a real dinosaur meaning "fused" or "bent
lizard." Those of us whose backbones
are gradually fusing.
Those of us who are slowly morphing
into the fluidity of the Tin Man.
Those of us in chronic pain
as each ligament and muscle
begins to tighten and harden as the spine
loses movement.
Those of us who would never take
simple things like checking blind spots,
or dressing for granted again,
if only we could travel in time and
evict earlier.

Thesis

My abuser was a young girl, who was also abused.
For years, I called her my best friend,
but that label was birthed more from
self-preservation, rather than truth.
She was tall, blond, thin, and a bit masculine.
Her parents divorced when she was an infant,
and she lived primarily with her wealthy father
and blended family. They traveled often to places
like New York City for Thanksgiving
and Aspen for Christmas.
She probably could have been a model, but chose
medical school for psychiatry instead.
She was smart-as-hell, the type who made straight As
without studying. The type that always started- and
finished- major projects the night before.

But me, I'm completely average.
Smart, but not quite smart enough for medical school
and certainly not the type that could finish a project
overnight. No, my major project of self-discovery
is years in the making. Years of unmasking
abuse and shedding layers right down
to the rainbow colors of me.

And my research questions go like this:

Am I looking for a woman to truly care for me
because this so-called-friend could not?

Am I trying to find my worth in a woman
because my abuser stole that
right along with my innocence?
Am I seeking a voice that sounds like silk and lacks
the coarseness of my abuser, who trades the vile
smell of her breath and the cheap Plugins that
saturated her room, with scents of clean linen and
warm perfumes, so I can feel feminine love rightly?

Are these the reasons I am searching,
or have these desires always been there
mixed and muddied by the shame of abuse
just waiting to be purified?

Ocean Friend

You haven't shared much about growing
up in one of Florida's beachside towns, but
I imagine you love the ocean because of it. And,
really, it would be no surprise to me, as your
ebbs and flows seemingly mirror
the ocean's highs and lows.

During our first dinner
(gourmet appetizers, fettuccine,
and Dark and Stormies), you shared
vulnerabilities—your difficulties making
friends, your desire for authenticity, and the
book with the line that would later change
my life, "If you own your stories, you get
to write the ending." As I left your
home, the co-dependency piece of
me whispered, "I could fix her."

As our friendship deepened, we
shared our secrets in the open spaces
between silence and tears. As salty droplets
puddled around us, blurring the intensity of our
gazes, it felt like our spot in the sand was
slowly giving way to the sea. Soon, I

was certain, we would wade together
chest-deep in the high tide.

One late spring night and one
full season after our first dinner, you
reached over and maternally caressed
my cheek with your fingertips. In that moment,
I felt as tethered to you as the moon to the sea.
But then, you retracted–looked away, crossed
your arms, and halted all reciprocity. I chased
this wave as far as I could, but it was
swallowed up by the deep, blue sea.
As I stood in the lowest of tides
willing it to return, I learned
the same wave never
crashes twice.

Almost a year after meeting,
we stood in your kitchen, our
feelings so hurt, causing an ocean
to fall from our eyes yet again. I was
afraid you would drift away forever, carried
off by the riptide. I offered life-raft after life-raft,
woven together with ropes of insecurity and
shame, praying you would grasp on. I
swam hard against the undertow, each
futile stroke pushing you further
away. Soon, I grew weary, and
I realized, it was my own

self that needed saving
before I drowned.

So, now I float, letting the gentle
current carry me with no particular
destination in mind. No fighting against
the waves as the water laps against my edges.
When the free-spirited piece of you is released—
the one with the nose ring and curls—
I hope you'll settle in close to me,
somewhere in the cradle of the
ocean's highs and lows.

Pure Poison by Dior

It's hard to know if I fell for your perfume or
friendship first. It's definitely the first thing I
noticed. I remember the day I asked if stealing a
girl's fragrance was the equivalent of stealing
another teen's prom dress, and I remember well
how ashamed I felt when you answered,
"You're a grown woman, wear what you want."
It was expensive, so I only bought a travel size.
I wore it often, even though it smelled slightly
different on me—
not as warm and enticing.
It's still my favorite scent though,
even long after you've left.
Sometimes I smell the bottle—
the scent lingering months after it emptied.
I want to buy more—this time a full bottle,
but I can't now,
because all I smell is you.

Doctor Friend

I reached for your hand as I fell to the ground
from my self-inflicted heart surgery.
As I cut each corroded artery pumping
the toxins of sexual abuse throughout my body,
I relied on you to hold the instruments—
your hands as steady as your friendship.
I thought you would be there, watching each
stitch heal, whispering encouragement as
I began to rise from the ash.
Instead, you walked away.
Leaving me there
bleeding out.

Haunting

The best part of this Friday the 13th
birthday of yours, is
for the first time in four years,
I had no desire to tell you
Happy birthday.

I did read your other friends' wishes on
social media, one of which included a picture
of you high in a skyrise in Tokyo dressed in
all back, seemingly enamored by two projected
ghosts dancing outside the windows.

You reached out to touch one, and I saw
your familiar and curious smile—
the one you used to give so freely—
spread across your face. The smile I thought I
knew so well that was the muse for all the
stories I had created—and cultivated—
in my head about our deep friendship.

For a second, I found myself wishing you back,
but then I remembered you never really came to
know and love my roots,
and I had only fallen for the
ghost of you anyway.

Ode to Carol

(You have to see the movie to understand)

Many, many years ago, as I walked
blindly through life, creatively motivated
without the action,
I met my own Carol.

Assertive, refined, classy, smart—
When she spoke,
she looked intently into my eyes, holding gaze
for seconds past the awkward stage.
Sometimes when we talked,
her hand would linger on my arm.
And then, one day, seemingly out of the blue,
she left, too.

And the movie ended for me.
But I have to wonder,
did the writers feel this, too?
Were they also heartbroken?
Instead of hoping, praying, and
escaping deep into fantasy of what could have
been, did they write their own happy ending?

Is creativity always birthed from such longing—
sewn from threads of relationships unraveling?

www.ingramcontent.com/pod-product-compliance
Lightning Source LLC
LaVergne TN
LVHW041241200726

843507LV00013B/2764